LETTERS TO OUR *Daughters*

A COLLECTION OF THOUGHTS, WISDOM, AND LIFE LESSONS FROM BLACK MOTHERS

COACH CAYME ANDREA

Written and collected by:
Cayme Andrea

Letters to Our Daughters
A collection of thoughts, wisdom & life lessons from Black mothers

Published by:
Leftwich & Lott Publishing, Charlotte, NC USA
Printed in the United States of America
First Printing Edition, November 2021
ISBN 978-0-578-87804-1

Edited by:
Allyson Elyse Garrett & Jessie Raymond
Photographer: Janelle Marie @janellemarieshoots
Book design by: Aeysha Mahmood

This book is dedicated to the following:

To my beautiful mother, Audrey Washington, and to the other two women with whom I have been blessed to call ma; Frances Watkins and Colesta Jackson. You have each poured so much into me and have shaped me into the woman and mother that I am today. I am grateful for your presence and influence in my life. I pray that I am as good a daughter to you as you are mothers to me.

To my daughter, Zavi Elyse. You continue to amaze me. You will always be my Chief Motivating Officer. I am so proud of you and the young lady you are growing into. You are love, light and greatness personified. Thank you for believing in me and leaving me encouraging notes in my office. You inspire me and challenge me to be better.

To my ancestors who continue to guide and watch over me, thank you for your unseen, but very real presence in my life. I am deeply grateful for the road that you paved and the sacrifices you made so I could be me. I AM because of YOU.

Contributing Authors:

Alease Acker
Ajiri Barnes
Audrey Washington
Carrianne Hilliard
Charlenea Duncan
Colesta Jackson
Delores Foster
Erica Frazier
Georgia Haywood
Iesha Treadwell
Jacqueline Brown
Jacquelyn Edwards-Wilson
Jasmine Ratliff
Karen Romaine Thomas
Kaz Wright
L'Monique King
La Vone Parks
Leslie Oliver
Margo Scurry
Mary Lewis
Melissa McQueen-Simmons
Melissa Morris
Myrna Key-Parker
Ronda Parks
Sandra Oliver
Shari Haywood
Sharita Meeks
Susan
TaNesha Barnes
Tawanna Francis
Theresa Prather-Harris
Tiffany Harrison
Unique Lee
Ursula Foster
Vondalyn McQueen-Simmons
Yvonne Harrison

CONTENTS

ACKNOWLEDGEMENTS

To my wife, Ronda, thank you for your constant support and the awesome ways in which you hold our family down and keep me grounded. You are an amazing mom in your own right and do a great job in nurturing, protecting, and guiding our little girl. I am often humbled by your strong belief in me and my dreams.

Thank you to all the mothers who submitted letters. Thank you for trusting me with your words and allowing the world to see and hear your heart.

About the Author

Cayme Andrea, affectionately known as Coach Cayme, is the founder of the Catalyst Coach Academy and CEO of Catalyst Global, LLC. She uses proven systems and methodologies to assist individuals in clarifying, creating, and sustaining successful outcomes, both personally and professionally. Coach Cayme believes in the connection of mind, body, and spirit and therefore takes an integrative approach to the work she does with clients. As an accredited coach and certified NLP practitioner with over 15 years in the industry, her education, training, experience, and spiritual insight make her a widely-sought after speaker, coach, and consultant.

@coachcayme

caymeandrea.com

INTRODUCTION

Letters to Our Daughters was born shortly after my daughter turned 2 years old. My wife gifted me with a set of leather bound, personalized journals and I started using them to write letters to my daughter and share my personal challenges and new levels of awareness. Initially, my goal was to turn these letters into a gift for her once she reached an appropriate age.

After a couple of years of writing in my journal, I felt this commitment was bigger than me and bigger than her. I realized that black and brown women everywhere who hadn't had the opportunity to have meaningful conversations with their mothers could benefit from the wisdom of other mothers of color. In 2018, I launched the project to invite women of color to share letters to their daughters. I put out an open call for submissions, and for the next 1.5 years, I received letters from these women, sharing lessons, advice, and suggestions on how to navigate life.

Hence, to my own daughter and to daughters everywhere - especially to our daughters of color - these pages are for you. Glean from the life lessons of mothers who are beautifully flawed and perfectly imperfect. Although we come from different backgrounds, have different experiences and social-economic statuses, one thing we have in common is that we share a deep intention of being the best mothers we can be, while using the tools we can access at different points in time.

While these letters are written to our specific daughters, the wisdom is being offered for you to consume. We noticed some letters had overarching themes, so we created categories in order for you to better be able to find a letter that would speak to a specific topic.

Absorb the insight. Find messages within the letters that resonate with you.

Open yourself to the words of healing, love, forgiveness, guidance, hope and instruction that await you, from the experienced great-grandmother, to the first-time foster mom. If the contents of these letters help you, even the least bit, then the mission of this project has been accomplished.

Inception Letter

To My Dear Zavi Girl,

I carried this personalized journal around with me for the last three months, trying to determine exactly how I wanted to use it. Then today, as I was sitting at my desk, waiting for my client to show up, I decided to seize the moment to write to you. This journal will be my letter to you. Perhaps when you turn 18 or 21, I'll give it to you. Your Tati gave me this as part of my Christmas present, so in some ways, this will be a present to both of us.

My prayer for you always, my precious angel, is that you realize you are strong enough to stand alone when you need to, smart enough to know when you need some help, and brave enough to ask for it.

Love,

Mami YaYa (Cayme Andrea)

CHAPTER ONE

Loving Self

Dear Cydney,

You are loved, I love you. God loves you. I can't believe how much I am enjoying being your mother. You challenge me in many ways. I cherish your fearless nature.

As you continue to grow, I want you to know that you will always have my full support in all that you do. I can't wait to see how you take on this world and make your mark. As your mother and your first female influence, I sometimes wonder if I am providing you with a true example of a strong woman figure. Although that question may pop up in my mind from time to time, your ongoing desire to spend time with me and the adventures that you don't mind taking in order for both of us to learn, make me smile.

I remember when you were only a few months old and we had to rush you to the hospital. I was so scared, but you seemed to look at me with assurance, as if to say that you were going to be fine. As I look at you now, I see that same confidence in your eyes.

As your mother, I've always wanted to have the opportunity to tell you how beautiful you are. There will be people that will come into your life that will tell you something different; don't listen. I want you to experience all of the love and respect that you deserve. Know that your happiness will come from you. Appreciate all of your blessings; never envy others for what you may perceive to be better. I'm certain that you will never settle for anything less than you deserve.

I Love You,

Mom (Charlenea)

My Sweet Gianna (Tink),

I love you so much and I am so proud to call you my daughter! You are my 'Baby girl' and my youngest child; you are the most sensitive and caring of my three children. I know that these first 10 years of your life have been tough, but mommy wants you to know that no matter what life brings, YOU ARE ENOUGH!

You have dealt with and overcome non-traditional approaches to your education, and you are handling it well. I know some days are more challenging than others, but keep moving forward. You received a medical diagnosis that would cause many to become very frustrated but, after you had an understanding of what you could do, you focused on moving forward. With all that you have experienced, you still remain focused on others. You put those you care about first and always want to ensure that those around you are okay.

As you journey through life, you may encounter individuals that may mistake your kindness for weakness, but that is not your issue; it is theirs, as it shows that they have some healing to do. Don't allow that to change your authentic self. You are beautiful with your peachy toned skin, coily hair, full lips and beautiful eyes. I know, at times, you struggle with loving and accepting the little girl you see when you look in the mirror, but I am here to tell you, "You are Enough!" You are smart (you learn differently), you are capable, you are organized, you are a planner, you love to dress fly (you get that from your grandma), you dance to the beat of your own drum, you care about others, you are empathetic, you are wise beyond your years and you are an evangelist in training.

If I could leave you with something, it would be this — do not allow the challenges you have encountered early in life define who you are. Allow them to shape you into who you are meant to be. Allow the challenges to become stepping stones along your life's journey, and not stumbling blocks. When you do stumble, pick yourself up, dust yourself off and keep moving forward.

When I was younger, I would focus on the challenges and begin to allow negative self-talk to ring loudly in my ears, to the point that all I believed was what I could not do instead of what I could do. You can do anything that you set your mind to, but it begins with believing in yourself. Oftentimes, you don't clearly understand my passion and the reasons that I push you to be great. I don't want you to become stuck, believing that you are incapable, and then begin looking for validation from others. That which you have passion for must come from within.

When I was younger, I was a chunky little girl, and I did not believe that I was beautiful, nor did I think I was capable. I wanted to be great, but didn't believe I was capable, and I didn't feel like I was enough. I didn't learn until adulthood that I am enough; strong enough, smart enough and beautiful enough. My hope for you is that you learn early in life that you are enough! Just as you are, YOU ARE ENOUGH!! Now, go and be great! I love you to infinity and beyond!

Love you bunches,

Mommy (Erica)

Dear Mi'Ana,

I loved you before I knew who you were; before I knew who I was. I had you as an adolescent, coming into adulthood. There were so many steps that I missed, and I did not realize it until I was raising you. Sometimes, I still beat myself up for the things that I did not do; for example, not opening up to you and letting you know who I am. Oftentimes, mothers are afraid to open up to their daughters because we are scared of the truth. We are quick to tell you not to hang out with the bad crowd (misunderstood due to circumstances) or date a certain person, or even question your choice in schools or careers, not because we know what's best, but because we survived through that very road you are traveling and so, we're wary on your behalf. There are so many things we have to watch out for as mothers, that we (I in particular) forget to have real conversations with you. We often get caught up in a lot of stuff, that we forget a major thing our daughters will benefit from — real conversations with their mothers. So, Mi'Ana, because I had so few real conversations with you, I am putting it here in this letter. It won't be the first or last letter (due to having received so many before), but it will be good for you to get this one as well.

Mi'Ana, thank you for choosing me to be your mother. Your life started off as a challenge. I have been fighting for you this entire time the best way I know how. First, I had to fight for my life and freedom to become an adult within my parents' home while trying to bring you into this world. Your mother was a grown little girl who was tired of so many wrong things happening within her family and community. I thought I was here to raise you, but you actually raised me to be the mom that I am today. I didn't understand life and the most important part of motherhood until you were deep into late elementary school. I had gone through so many phases like depression, low self-esteem and low self-worth, valuing other people's opinions of me - over my own - because of a number of things I was exposed to as a child, leading into adulthood. I didn't realize the effects it would have on you; I thought if I could merely provide for you financially, all would work out.

We, as mothers, hold ourselves accountable for all that we've done and we push so hard for our daughters to be better than us. However, we neglect to teach them how to overcome our struggles and have those real conversations with them. Eventually, I started having these conversations with you, and, midway through high school, we started putting the broken pieces together. I did not know that we both had so many broken pieces as a result of my actions. Mothers, it is very important to teach our daughters how they should be treated regardless of how you feel about yourself.

Now that I know better, I do better. I teach you more by letting you figure it out - with little help from me, and more from God - while having those real conversations. That's why I pushed you away to college. I wanted you to learn more and understand more about yourself than anything else, so that you could begin to make better decisions than I did when I was the same age. I am sometimes unable to relate because our paths are so different, but I know communication is key. I know that when we spend time together, it is better because we both take the time to understand each other. I also know that you are a fighter because both of your parents are fighters and leaders. We do not take any mess from anyone, and likewise, I've raised you to be a leader and to fight for your rights, with God being in charge.

Mi'Ana, you are a wonderful young lady that should be proud of all the things you have had to overcome to be who you are becoming. Know that your story does not end badly. You are just getting started, and what a wonderful way to do so. Continue on your journey with God and let him heal you, now, instead of later, like I am doing. Each experience builds a memory of what was, but you have to look into what will be. Life has taught me quite a few personal lessons that have been outlined in my book. The most important lesson is to be true to yourself and plan how you want to spend your life. Always have SMART goals and plan for risks and failures; although they may hurt you, they will make you stronger. Prepare to get the worst while you are young, so that as you grow, there will be less bitterness and disappointment. Don't ever give up on your dreams! Family, friends and all kinds of people will put their disappointments on you, but you got this…so, stay focused!

Do your research on yourself, have dates with yourself, try new things and explore life. Life has more to offer than what you see. Continue to wait on having a little you. Men will always be here, so, choose wisely and take your time. At your age, most guys are simply having fun. Keep those high standards and don't compromise to please another, or you will end up being mad at yourself. I didn't plan to be a single mom, but that's how things turned out. Get the degree you want, not what you think I want for you. It is okay to change your mind, but look into the details with the end in mind.

In other words, start your plan with the end results in mind; you can do this by asking more questions to others in your industry and letting God lead you. Don't worry about those who doubt you; stay away from those crazy professors and peers. Instead, connect with positive people who believe in your creativity. The truth is what you tell yourself. When you believe that all things are possible, they will be. The truth is what is in your mindset, according to your own greatness. Know that no one is perfect, although some of us try hard to be. Be you, and you will be fine.

Go forth and change the world with our designs. You have been designed to be here at this time, for this reason. So, my only question is, will you continue to go further into your purpose and destiny for your life?

I love you and wish that God's will would be manifested in you; favors and blessings will surround you all the days of your life.

Love you,

Mom (Carrianne)

My Dearest Gabrielle (Nooty),

I love you deeply, and I am so proud to call you my daughter. You are my first-born daughter and your personality is the closest to mine. You are quick-witted (smart-mouthed), focused on your education, and at 13 years of age, you have a plan (unlike me when I was your age). You are sensitive, caring, silly, make those closest to you smile and laugh and, more importantly, you love your family. You have wonderful qualities that will carry you into adulthood and enable you to be a wonderful friend, and - if you choose - wife and mother.

My message to you is, YOU ARE ENOUGH! Just as you are the good and the bad, you are enough. Don't ever let anyone make you think you have to change your authentic self to fit in or belong. As life continues, there will come a time when you think you have to change who you are to fit; don't do it. Be yourself, you are beautiful, wise beyond your years and smart. When challenges come - and they sure will - remember my voice in your head, saying, "You are enough and you got this!"

Your full lips, your coily hair, your milk chocolate skin and almond-shaped eyes make up your beauty on the outside. However, it is your charm, intelligence, care, sensitivity, focus, determination, vision, silliness, observation and kindness that are the qualities that make you beautiful on the inside. Always love yourself first, more than you love others. This way, you will not spend your life trying to find someone to love and appreciate you because that love will come from within.

When I was younger, I never felt like I was enough. I didn't feel smart or pretty, and I wasted many years looking for validation, love and approval from others. Don't do that. It took mommy a long time to earn to love myself, to love my looks and believe that I am smart and capable. I am committed to telling you, every day that I breathe, "You are smart, beautiful and capable of anything you put your mind to." Learn to hear positive self-talk: the voice in your head that drowns out all other messages you hear. That voice should say, "You can do this, Gabby, you are beautiful, Gabby, you are smart Gabby, you don't have to compromise, Gabby, and you are an overcomer, Gabby."

Right now, as a 13-year-old, you are preparing to enter high school, playing travel basketball and have set a life plan for yourself to attend college on a scholarship, play ball overseas or in the WNBA and have a career that involves sports in some capacity. Remain focused and determined because friends will come and go, but your choices will affect your life for years to come. Now, don't get me wrong, don't go through life in fear, just be mindful of the choices you make because they have consequences; some, good and some, bad. Whatever you do in life, always remember that I love you just the way you are. And you are more than capable of doing anything you set your mind to. I love you more than this letter may express!

Love you bunches,

Mommy (Erica)

In a mother's words…

"YOU ARE ENOUGH!"

My Spirited Daughter,

It's the beginning of the new year and I've already started learning lessons!

Listen, you are a stubborn, strong-willed child, and that's an AWESOME trait to have. It really is a strength! Remember this though — a strength overdone becomes a weakness.

One of the lessons I've learned as regards loving someone else and being in a loving relationship is to know when to drive your stake in the ground (and die on it if you must) and when to yield. Getting your way all the time is a very lonely experience. Another way to put this is: You can be right and be happy, but sometimes, you have to prioritize the most important choice, depending on the moment.

Here are a few other lessons that the Universe has really driven home to me this year:

- You must always be true to yourself!
- Don't force situations or circumstances. Let them play out naturally, and be wise enough to see the outcome for what it is, when it happens.
- A person can't love you and treat you any better or at any higher level than they love and treat themselves.

The same goes for you, so, make sure that you treat yourself with the same level of love and respect you want someone else to show you.

I love you, my angel. I may not have made all the right choices or all the choices that would have yielded the best outcomes, but when I knew better, I did better.

Had I been strong enough to stand in my truth and own my own power, there are certain things that I would've done differently for you, not only when you were born, but also, in the early years of your life. Now, I acknowledge that I know better, and upon recognizing my power to choose and create the life I desire, I now do better! Hindsight is 20/20.

One of the hardest lessons that I had to learn was that it's ok to disappoint another to be true to yourself. My hope for you is that it doesn't take you until you're in your 40's before you get that.

With all the love my heart can hold for you,

Mami (Cayme Andrea)

To Angel and Ashley,

I was so young when I had you both, so, in reality, we all grew up together. When I was pregnant with both of you, I thought I had things figured out and knew where I was going. I know I wasn't perfect, but I think we three made a pretty good team. In growing as a mother while growing into a woman, there have been so many life lessons that I've learned, most of which I haven't shared with you up until now.

See, you're both adults and mothers now, so you already know that there is a certain amount of readiness you have to arm yourself with every day. You have to be ready for the crazy questions the kids will come up with, and you also have to be prepared for messes and boo-boos. But those aren't the lessons that will help you grow as a woman. Sure, the kids will appreciate it and you'll feel good, some of the time, as a parent; but what I want you to know most of all, is that you are so much more than what you are right now.

As a woman, as a black woman, you represent the strength of all the women who came before you and made a difference in this world. You have a collective wisdom in spirit that is with you always, just waiting to be tapped into. I'm not talking about a God or Goddess or an ethereal third party. I'm saying that within your soul, you have every answer to every question you could ever come up with. If you can learn to be silent and listen to yourself, you will change the world as you know it.

I know you're thinking, "OK mom, you're getting a little too mystical right now," but just hear me out. I can tell you every day how amazing you are and how you can be anything you want to be, but if you don't hear yourself saying it, you will never live up to your greatness. You have to believe that you CAN create your dreams. If you listen - and I mean, truly listen to your inner voice - without doubt, without judgement and without interference, you will hear what your higher purpose is.

Now I'm not going to tell you this is easy, as that would be a lie; in fact, it will be the hardest thing you ever do. But what is life for, if not to live it to your fullest potential? See, nothing is more important than you discovering who you were meant to be, and no one can define who that is except you. You only have NOW to be happy.

I can admit that until very recently, I haven't followed this advice. This is partly because I was more focused on others than on myself, and I thought it was the noble thing to do. But in truth, it was mostly because I didn't truly understand how amazing I was and how I had been neglecting you and the rest of the world, by not shining my light. Knowing what I know now, I'm here to tell you that you don't need to wait anymore; you have everything you need to be the best you that you can be.

Finally, I want to tell you a few things to avoid while you start putting in the work. Don't let yourself get in the way of your dreams. This means that you shouldn't talk yourself out of being amazing. Don't ever get so comfortable in your life that you decide that you've done enough. Keep stretching for more. Don't ever believe you aren't worthy of greatness. Make a constant reminder to yourself every day, "I deserve the best that life has to offer. I deserve to find my purpose in life." This was a great piece of advice from Les Brown.

Know that I love you more than you could ever know, and that you need to love yourself just as much.

Mom (Melissa M.)

Dear Lailah,

I am writing you this letter to let you know that you are enough. You are more than enough. Although the world has thrown you some hard punches, you always manage to conquer them with such grace and strength. I am so inspired by your strength, grit and confidence in yourself (and mostly, God). You don't know how to talk, but you praise and worship God. You don't know how to walk but you know that your steps are ordered by God; step away, baby, God's got you. You've shown me so much these past 6 years. You've shown me unconditional love, patience, grace, forgiveness, hope and faith. You have strengthened my relationship with God, and for that, I thank you.

Our life is not what we thought it would be, but I wouldn't want it any other way. You are one of a kind (literally, because your syndrome is 1 in 35,000). Don't ever forget that God has chosen you. He chose us. God has chosen us so that he can do a great work in us that can be projected into the world. This work was predestined before either of us was born. Your life is meant to show people what healing, grace and mercy looks like through Christ. Jeremiah 1:5 states, "I knew you before I formed you in the womb. Before you were born, I set you apart." Lailah, I believe this with all my heart.

I want you to know that you are loved so much, regardless of your "disability." You are strong, you are my best friend and I love you with all my heart. Mommy's prayer for you is that you continue to seek the Lord, lead others to Jesus, keep your head up towards the sky and live in your calling. I promise, I will be here every step of the way.

God Bless You, Queen.

You are Loved.

Alease

Dear Zoe,

First and foremost, let me tell you how much I love and adore you. I'm beyond proud to be your mother and honored that God saw fit to intertwine our lives.

I've learned so much in these last almost 43 years of living and so, I want to share a few of my life lessons with you that will prayerfully help you navigate through this thing we call life. I'm not perfect; I've never claimed to be. There may have been decisions that I made that weren't the best, choices I made that weren't the smartest, thus, I want to seize this opportunity to apologize for anything that I didn't do, or things that I could've done better.

First, you are beautiful. Always stay in-tune with your inner beauty. This has nothing to do with physical appearance but everything to do with whom God created you to be. You are creative. You are kind. You are wise. You are generous. You are loving. This is who you are, and because of that, God will make sure you attract what and who you are. Be sure to love yourself first, love who God created you to be, love who God designed you to be. You are a very unique individual, and because of your ability to give life, many will be attracted to you. Never forget that you are worthy and valuable. Your worth is not attached to things or people, but to your ability to remain true to yourself and your creator. God has enabled you to love others selflessly. Your name Zoe, in the Greek, means "to give life." You will be blessed because you love unconditionally. When you love yourself, you can love others without hesitation.

You have a heart just like your Mommy; it's big, it's caring, it's generous, it's consistent and it's forgiving. God has chosen us to love everyone, no matter what manner of life they've been presented with. Mommy always wants you to spoil people with love, including those you like, those you don't like, those who look like you and those who don't. The greatest gift you've been given is love; I pray you love people the same.

Second, I always want you to feel a sense of pride in who you are. You're not perfect, but you are purposeful. God created you with purpose, and you are special, unique and more than enough. Don't minimize your worth, your value or your calling in life. Don't doubt yourself, don't doubt your abilities, don't doubt what God has given you. Stay in-tune with yourself. Set your expectations, and do not lower them for yourself or for others. Whatever you desire to do, pursue it with dignity, character and integrity.

Lastly, always keep God first, at the center of your life. Don't make decisions without using discernment. Trust God in everything you do. Trust God in your friendships and your relationships. Trust God even when you can't trace him. There's one more thing you will need to live a fruitful life, and that's FAITH! Place your faith in God, not people. Cultivate faith, and when you lack or need more, ask it of God. Allow your faith to lead you to uncharted territories. Your future is just as bright as your big, beautiful eyes. Reach for the stars! The world is better with you being in it.

I love you,

Mommy (Yvonne)

In a mother's words...

"NO ONE IS PERFECT."

Dear Camdyn LaVon,

You are beautiful. You are loved. You will be great. You will be creative.

You will be disciplined but you will have a free spirit.

"We will give you everything you need to be YOU."

This is the mantra we said to you while I carried you for the forty weeks and five days. These are the words we say to you now in hopes that they will be embedded in your BEING as you journey through this world.

You were created with an abundance of intention in a world that has not always protected black or brown people, women nor children as best it could. We had encountered ecstatic joys and heartbreaking valley lows which prepared us for you. We have faith that this world will be better prepared for such a being as you. We wanted a child to share our love, our resources and our joy of loving and living life to the fullest. We believe that you chose us to be your parents because we have everything you need to survive and prosper in this world. Also, we created you a village of like-minded people that would navigate this life with you, protect you and provide you with even more love, support and wisdom. We will provide you with a firm spiritual foundation. We both have experienced wars in our lifetime in hopes that you won't have to. We know that you are uniquely ours and we are ready. The world has grown to be much more inclusive as we have aged, and with all of the social justice work taking place in our communities, we believe there is hope for you to be or become whoever you want to be.

Remember, you have all of the resources you need to survive. Don't allow fear to control your thoughts or your actions. Keep God first and rest assured that God is always speaking! Our ancestors watch over us like angels and look out for us in ways in which others do not have the capacity. Know that we (your mothers) will protect you, teach you, nurture you, lead you and love you with everything we have!

With love,

Your Mommies (Melissa and Vondalyn)

To: My Izzy Boo, LaLa Mama, Baby Ava & Evie

Hello my loves,

I want to take a moment to share a little bit about life. Now, your mothers are amazing women and have been amazing parents, though they aren't perfect — well, neither are you. I know they have taught you so many beautiful lessons that you are already brimming with love and greatness. Be kind to them because they have spent years equipping you with the skills to become tremendous women, and they have also sacrificed a lot of themselves to do everything they can for you. Also, keep in mind that they were raised by a pretty amazing woman, so, remember that Mima is here to answer the tough questions your mothers may not have answers to just yet, including one big secret.

Life isn't fair! I start with this because you will probably spend a good portion of life wondering why something did or didn't happen, and asking where fairness is. Fairness isn't something to strive for because fairness doesn't exist. Fairness is in the eye of the beholder, and no two persons see it through the exact same lens.

Instead of fairness, figure out what is best for you. Be clear about what you are willing to accept or what you are willing to fight to change. You are the only person that you have any control over, so you have to be the 'star' in the movie that is your life.

The biggest lesson I can share with you is to put yourself first! From now until the end of your days as a woman, putting yourself first will not be something that is taught to you very often. In our society, we teach girls especially, that they have to think of the group, take care of others and make room for those who need help. I'm here to tell you that you won't be able to do any of those things effectively, until you are comfortable with the person you choose to be. If you aren't happy, fulfilled or even doing things you enjoy, your ability to help anyone else will fall short, and you will never grow. If you aren't willing to think of yourself first, why would anyone else? This means that you have to understand who you are before you can help anyone else.

You will have relationships with friends, family, partners and coworkers that will sometimes be great, and sometimes, be heavier than you think you can bear. All you can do is focus on what's best for you in every situation. Ask yourself lots of questions about everything in your life; don't take anything for granted or become complacent. Ask yourself, "Is this friend someone who is encouraging me to be better and listening to me like I listen to them? Is this partner here for me because they need me or because they want me? Does this job lead me to a place I want to go, or am I here just because it's comfortable or it's important to someone else?"

Never stop asking yourself, "What more can I be doing and what's the next step for me?" This isn't about being selfish or not caring for others, this is about creating the best version of yourself to share with the world.

There are so many things I hope to share with you over your lifetime. Making sure you are the best version of yourself is just the beginning.

Love,

Mima (Melissa M.)

Dear Solana,

One of the most painful lessons I have ever learned resulted in your life. Every single tear was worth it. You made me a God among goddesses, and a warrior. But the pain I endured, I desperately hope you can avoid. I labored over all the important things I've always wanted to share with you in this letter, but I settled for talking to you about self-possessed womanhood, men, love, sex and self-worth. No one spoke to me about these things, and it left me vulnerable. Therefore, I vowed to myself that you would know.

I am watching you blossom into your early stages of womanhood. I love watching how gracefully you move, how beautifully your body is developing and how self-aware you are of your own power. NEVER let someone take that from you. This body of yours is YOURS. Own it. Protect it. Defend it. Choose with a clear heart and mind who you will share it with. It will serve as a vessel of creativity and strength as you move through the world.

If you are anything like your mama, you will like boys. They will be interesting to you. You will like how you affect them. You may even want to explore them. When this happens, you should know a few things; some technical and some emotional.

Remember this when you begin to give in to this natural phase of life — boys and girls move differently. While girls are thinking about love, boys are thinking about sex. Women are built with a hormone called oxytocin. It makes you feel amazing. It generates feelings of love, trust and connection. When it rushes our body, you will think the boy in front of you is the most wonderful thing the universe created. He may be. He may not.

However, your body will no longer be in your own control; this is not the same for boys. So, it will be crucial to move very slowly to touch. The worst thing that can happen is that your body will betray you and give space to someone who is unworthy of your time, attention and affection. Always remember that sex and love are not the same thing. You may be having sex in love, while they, on the other hand, may merely be having sex.

My first sexual experience was when I was quite young. I am not afraid to tell you this. It was beautiful. It was filled with kindness, sweet letters and grand acts of love. No matter when it happens for you, my love, my greatest desire is that it will be the same; full of admiration, respect, surprise and safety. I want your heart to be filled and all your affections, returned. Love, sex and life are to be enjoyed. Live, my love, just remember that women have all the power and control. You make your own choices; I would just like to plead with you to take your time to make sure that these boys will leave you whole.

I am raising you to be a free woman. Know that the world is not kind to us. You will have to fight to express your most powerful self. Fight. There will be the woman the world wants you to be and there will be the woman you actually are. Trust yourself. You tell the world who you are; you don't let the world define you. With that said, know that the choices you make will all come with social consequences.

From what I have observed, men all over the world love the free woman. He will absorb all of her fire and drown in every adventure she possesses; but he may not see this woman as worthy of marriage and partnership. This may be out of control, sometimes from jealousy and, mostly, out of sexism. You will have to decide for yourself if that means anything to you, and move accordingly. But no matter what, keep moving and keep growing. Don't let anyone put you in a box based on their intellectual, religious or social limitations.

Be clear. Communication will be your most valuable tool. Many times, as women, we move in a situation according to what we FEEL. Make sure you have not created a fantasy of what you want it to be. Make sure you ask questions until you are satisfied. Make sure his intentions are clearly stated. Hear EXACTLY what he says and not what you want to hear. Make sure that what is actually being offered is what you want to choose. This will save you, my love. This will empower you. Be in control of your own choices, and you will never be the victim.

Please know that if you are to ever choose a man that harms you in any way, the man will not be chastised for his bad behavior. We don't teach men to be better people. They will hold you accountable for not protecting yourself from harm. So, protect yourself you must.

Even with all these lessons, allow yourself to get lost in love. It will be the most beautiful experience you will ever have. I have loved and been loved many times. I have seen forever love. I have seen deep betrayal. I honestly wish I could guarantee you that solid romantic love exists for everyone, but the truth is, I am not sure. I'd like to add here that this is not to say that you should guard your heart so much so that you shut love out completely, as it is only through the loving of another person that we discover ourselves. What I am sure of, however, is that it is all a risk. If you do not take it, you have not lived. If by chance, your love is not reciprocated, appreciated or honored, allow that man to go. Keep your heart and spirit light. Love will come again.

What I learned from your birth is that the real pain lies in our inability to accept what has happened. Once I accepted that, I became stronger than I even knew possible. I realized the greatness in the possibility of what we could create together; you and I, mother and child. Apparently, heartbreak has its place too. But as a mother, I would rather you have the least pain possible. So, this is my attempt to be honest with you, to create a play book that does not dictate who and how you should be, but gives you pieces of what I learned the hard way. Trust me, brokenness is not an easy phase to recover from. Don't let anyone take pieces of you that you cannot recover. If by chance you get broken along the way, as all humans do, I will be right there to help put all the pieces back together again.

In love,
Solana's mama (TaNesha)

In a mother's words...

"YOU ARE THE MOST IMPORTANT PERSON ON THIS PLANET."

CHAPTER TWO

Forgiveness

Peace in the midst of a storm

Little girls are sugar and spice, so they say. But how did my little girl become so bitter and angry? Perhaps it was the shift in our family dynamics, or some indirect pressure from trying to live up to being my only surviving child. I have been asking myself this question repeatedly over the last several months, and I still have no simple answer. Life, womanhood, blackness and parenting are not simple. It's a mixture of you, me, past and present blended into a stew that either nourishes the soul or poisons it.

As a mother, sometimes it is hard to see your baby as a woman, even when you give your all to prepare her for womanhood. That is what I assumed I had done in her 20-plus years of life. I encouraged her to speak her truth; put herself first through self-love and challenge the status quo (which she did, even in middle school). Yet, in the midst of my encouragement, she became a person that I no longer recognized. I was so hurt that she would turn on me after I supported her in every way, even in times when I did not completely agree or understand.

The biggest lesson I've learned is that no one is perfect; there are no perfect parents, neither are there perfect ways to parent. When I became a mother, I had more compassion for my own mother. I then understood many things that she felt as a woman and mom that I simply could not relate to while growing up. We try not to pass on any past trauma to our daughters, but something always seems to seep through the cracks.

Certain situations can happen in families that can impact their lives. I resolve not to carry her burden of bitterness and anger. Instead, I will keep my arms and heart open for when she is ready.

The bottom line is, I miss my sweet girl. She has changed but I continue to envision a bright future for us; one filled with joy, love and most of all...forgiveness.

-Ursula

Dear Jada,

As I sit here missing my mom terribly, I reflect on all the things that I didn't get to know about her and how I wish I better understood her. Growing up, she never told me that she loved me, she never hugged me and she never kissed me. But then, I knew she loved me because that's an innate trait of a mother. When I think of her, the one thing that emanates, mostly, is that she was a God-fearing woman, and if I was ever in need of prayer, she was my go-to. So, now I ask, how will you remember me? How do I want you to remember me? What about my life can I impart on you in hopes of leaving you with words of wisdom that may be impactful?

My guess is that you see me as a "strong, educated, successful, black woman" because that is what I have allowed you to see. I haven't allowed you "in" to be able to see the vulnerable side; in fact, very few have. It's deflected by me making people feel that they need me, when in fact, I have this insatiable desire to feel needed; consequently, I extend myself beyond capacity. I do it with work, I do it with friendships, and I do it with family. That's not a healthy balance to life at all, because it destroys relationships. I implore you to learn early in life who is deserving of you. You can't be everything to everybody, and not everyone is deserving of the generous gift you can give; the gift of time and love. I was always afraid of not being liked and not being included. People will either like and respect you for who you are or they won't. I made the mistake of gifting my time to the wrong people, thinking that it would satisfy my desire of feeling needed, when actually, I was sacrificing my time with you. Yes, I was there, physically, for the cheerleading events, school lunches, girl scouts and basketball games (LOL), but I robbed you of my emotional presence. I spoke the words, "I love you" (unlike my mother) but I continued the cycle. I continued the cycle of not gifting you with me, and for that, I am sorry.

As black women, we are taught that you MUST be strong, but I'm here to tell you that it's okay to be SOFT. It's okay to show love, it's ok to show vulnerability and it's okay if we can't be superwomen. Learn to love unconditionally and learn to receive love and be kind to those who love you. Had this been the principle that governed my life, you and I would have been much closer. I would not have shielded my emotions. If I had a do over, we would have prayed together more often, and I would not have waited until you were 20 years old to build a friendship with you. If throughout your life, my lack of emotional presence left you feeling lonely, I'm sorry. Know that I love you unconditionally, and during your childhood, I loved you the only way I knew how.

I say all of this in hopes that one day, you will have the opportunity to do better than I did. The cycle won't be broken overnight, but it can get better with each generation. I love you, my sweet baby, and please know that I am here for you during my remaining days on this earth. I remember a heated conversation between us as if it was yesterday; you said that I didn't know you. You were right.

Hello, my name is Mom. Can we be friends?

I love you.

Karen

In a mother's words...

"LEARN TO LOVE UNCONDITIONALLY, LEARN TO RECEIVE LOVE AND BE KIND TO THOSE WHO LOVE YOU."

CHAPTER THREE

Dear L' Monique,

Mommy thought she would put the many thoughts and memorable moments of you in a letter to convey her true feelings to one of the finest daughters a mommy could have the pleasure of being connected to on this planet earth. There are so many experiences, as well as memories too innumerable to share. However, I will attempt to begin by engaging you in those which I will never forget, as they remain in my heart forever.

Looking back, when I realized that I was pregnant, my greatest wish was hoping that the pregnancy would produce a girl child. I still remember that when I finally gave birth, my first words were, "What did I have?" When I was told the baby was a girl, I was elated. My response: "I can't wait to tell my husband!" I got just what I had wished for, and to this day, my happiness has been immense.

Now that you have reared two sons and are currently caring for a deceased girlfriend's son, you are now being challenged for your skills, patience and endurance of parenting once again. Your sons are presently adults, and I feel so good about the fact that you can now call on them to assist you in conveying the importance of respect, integrity and education to the young man you're now rearing; I'm sure you do too.

Parenting is one of the most difficult jobs a mother is faced with, especially when your children are grown and you're looking forward to having time for yourself. This does not mean that you are not always there for your offspring, but at this point in life, when you've been freed from many of the responsibilities of rearing young children, you should have your time. Instead, you've chosen to honor a commitment to a lifelong friend by rearing her child. It is commendable, but please remember, you are a person too. You are the most important person on this planet. If you fall apart in your efforts to help someone else, no one benefits. Keep this in mind if the situation ever becomes an insurmountable one.

Let Mommy apprise you of how very proud of your academic accomplishments she is; graduating from college, attempting to acquire your Master's Degree, while working at an AIDS (testing, awareness and resource) facility. My feeling is quite intense about your involvement in this facility, realizing how many folk need to be informed of the physical knowledge of this life-threatening disease. I need not fail to mention that you are also teaching in a high school setting. This is yet another reason why Mommy is so very proud of your accomplishments and applauds your involvement in both areas of employment and productivity. As your grandmother so aptly articulated: 'Everything happens for a reason," which I truly believe, as you have proven it to be true. You are a caring/concerned individual with a heart of gold when it comes to helping family and friends.

I trust this letter has informed you of the love I carry in my heart for you while journeying on this planet earth. Mothers and their children don't always agree, however, at the end of the day we are still family. All things considered, I am so pleased to hear you call me Mommy. You are a beautiful daughter outwardly as well as inwardly. Loving you always!

Very truly yours,

(Delores)

Just a quick note to you,

My Dear Darling:

When you grow up and have the family (3 kids) that you say you want and dream about (as I write this to you even now at 45 years old), please, remember that Karma is real *insert devilish grin*. You woke me up several times last night because you wanted me to put the covers on you that you kicked off. This, however, was only after screaming and crying at the top of your lungs because I wouldn't get out of bed and come sit on the edge of your bed so you could lay on my lap and go back to sleep. In your crazy, tantrum-state, you wanted me to sit up all night in a specific spot on the bed so you could lay on me and be comfortable. You were so delirious that I actually felt sorry for you. I was so incredibly tired and frustrated with you, but I sat on the edge of my bed and rubbed you until you calmed down. You eventually got back in your bed on your own and went to sleep.

I pray you never lose the ability to be in touch with what you need at any given moment.

And I pray your emotional maturity and ability to communicate continue to improve so you can express your expectations and desires in a way that is respectful to you and those around you.

Mami (Cayme Andrea)

Dear Maya,

You are my only child, the special "one" that God created for my temporary care. When you were just a few days old, I lifted you to the skies and gave you back to the Lord for His blessings and guidance. I, my daughter, was chosen to nurture you for His plans for your life, and for that, I am immensely grateful.

In all of your endeavors - whether life-changing or small - keep God at the forefront of your aspirations. Ask Him for spiritual and moral discernment to make wise choices, to ensure that they align with the plans that He has for your life.

(Memorize Proverbs 3:5-6.)

Always remember that you must stand for something (what you believe in) lest you fall for anything. Be intentional about doing the right thing, especially when it is not popular, and you will be blessed.

Love you,

Mommy (Jacquelyn W)

Dear Camille,

I want to take this opportunity to tell you that I love you, and God loves you. You are my sweet, creative lover of learning. Despite that you have grown up to 12 years of age, I still can't believe that I am your mother. I often find myself thinking about my influence in your life. I truly pray that I have and will continue to be someone that you can say helped you to become a strong, intelligent and kind woman.

Please, know that no one is perfect and that there is always room for learning. As I think about having the opportunity to continue to watch you grow, I also want you to know that you deserve all the happiness that your beautiful heart desires. There will be people that will come into your life to try to alter your positive course, but I implore you to stay in your path.

With respect to boys, how I wish I could handpick the special someone for you, but I can't. However, I can teach and show you how you should be treated with respect as a woman. Please know that your happiness is based on your belief, not anyone else's.

Lastly, you are a precious gift that I cherish every single day. My life would not be complete without you. You have challenged me to look at the woman that I am and how I can continue to grow to encourage you.

I love you,

Mom (Charlenea)

My Dearest Judah,

I discovered that you were coming on a Friday evening in December 2001. I was excited for me, but afraid for you. This world isn't kind, despite how beautiful it is. But still, I had faith that you joining me in this world would give it more color; more light. As I first held you the night you were born, I wept for the moments that you would see rain upstage the sunshine and the times when you would first feel pain in your heart. I kissed your tiny hands and feet, and prayed to God to spare you. It was a selfish petition but I prayed it anyway.

As the years traveled past, I'd watch you sleep and hold on to my selfish prayer. God would meet me in the middle and show me that you were covered. Your questions to me and your observations of your world surprised and challenged me to release you; to let you find your own paths in the concrete. You, my rose, bloomed and bled, curled up against your fears and cried, danced and dared others to stop you. Sometimes, I fought for you; other times, I pushed from afar. You were never alone; I was always a shoulder behind. I am now just a breath away.

You took my everyday 'I love yous' and turned them into yourself. They shape our essence in the same way that you walk among the living, pronounce your intent and the way you style your growing 'fro' and eyebrows. You are truth, becoming and knowing. You are freedom, declaring devotion to yourself in your Converses and bedroom piles of teenage life. You are love; embracing our friends and your own ideologies. You are aware that the world isn't kind. You bring it light and color. You have become my prayer answered, yet, not without your own moments of darkness and its blues. While you haven't been spared, you have been blessed to see the sunshine even as the rain approaches.

Judah, you are evolving past my dreams and wishes. You have an ownership of yourself that I could never envision, but you still have much more to see and endure. While my early prayers were based on fear, your ordered steps have sharpened my faith. I held you so close at the beginning of your life that I forgot one key ingredient to life and motherhood — that you belong to God first. The more I trusted God as a mother, the more I became free to watch you fly.

While I am here to catch you as your wings tire amidst the wind, I know that God will lift and carry both of us. Always remember to fly; whether the wind is light, the sun is out, whether your wings are weary or your heart is heavy. Let the love God gifts us both with, every morning, remind you of how blessed you are, and never forget that my love will cover your life as God covers mine. You inspire me to be greater; your life is the evidence that God answers prayers. I love you from every cavern within my soul. Remember to fly humbly, and that I'm looking forward to that condo and Jaguar when you take over the world.

For now, I'm watching and backing you up from our skybox at home. I did your grind; I stand (lol). You got me. Forever. You're the best kid; on everything.

Je T'aime,

Mom (Leslie)

Dear Shawna,

How to write a letter to my beautiful daughter? When thinking about this, I did not imagine how difficult it would be. This is my opinion of motherhood: no one prepares you for this. I was a single mother when my daughter was born. Scared, lonely, alone and at 22 years of age, I had yet to experience what the world had in store for me and had no clue what to do. To my surprise, after 15 hours of labor, this bundle of joy (7 lbs. 2 oz and 20 inches long) with a head full of jet-black hair looking like a China Doll, came with the following instructions: 'HANDLE WITH CARE.' I named her Shawna Marie Harris; her middle name is after my loving mother. Taking her home from the hospital, I had no idea what to expect. You actually helped me become a woman.

Through the trials and tribulations of being your mother, you were the one to love me unconditionally, without preconceived notions or knowing right from wrong. As you grew from baby to girl, I watched your mind and body flourish to this beautiful person that God created, and all was well. Watching your journey in this thing called life - your years, and transitioning from girl to teenager and from teenager to woman - has been both exciting and challenging at times.

Shawna, all I can say is, "well done" and how proud I am of you. God has granted so many of my wishes for you. He has blessed you and kept you. He sent you the love of your life and you have your own family now. God has continued to remain in the center. With that being said my darling, through your tears, laughter, heartaches, disappointments and triumphs, just know that you're still my little girl, no matter what. May life continue to bless you and keep you as God has blessed me with you.

Your loving mother,
Theresa

Dear Cayla,

You are one of the best (along with your brother) and most successful creations in my life. I know you will experience challenges and some pain as you learn and grow. I wish to give you all of myself so that you don't make the same mistakes or path detours I made in order to attain happiness and fulfilment from life and get what I was deserving of. I struggled earlier in life with lack of confidence, not feeling included, loving myself and finding love. After all these years, it is only now that I've learned to accept myself and not let anyone make me feel 'less' or undeserving of what I want. Focus on the positive, your strengths and living in the now, in order to change the negative thoughts in your mind. They are just that — negative thoughts, to keep you from your goals, your true self and living your best life.

Although I had a great stable childhood with loving parents, there are things that shaped my thoughts, and now, I'm learning to recognize them in order to propel forward. I'm sharing this with you now so that you are always connected to your greatness. Don't allow anyone to define you by the color of your skin or your multicultural heritage. You possess all of these cultures to make you stronger, more unique and increase what you have to offer this world. Be smart; if it doesn't feel right, move into another direction. Know that you will be faced with hard decisions, and at times, life-altering decisions that may be necessary to make. Make them, regroup yourself, focus on your mind and thoughts and then move forward in faith.

I've learned so much from you; being open-minded, laughing at myself and just being me. I know that all of the things I have taught you up until now will give you the tools you need to create your own wonderful life experiences. Live your passion, use your strengths and show compassion to others. Don't dwell on the past, and more importantly, don't let the little word 'fear' get in your way. It did for me, too often, and crippled me. It is perfectly okay to pause or hesitate, but take the leap anyway, if it is what you want and if that leap gets you closer to your dreams. DREAM; put a plan in place to reach it and it will become a reality. So, DREAM. I can tell you this with all the truth and conviction from my soul. Believe in God, exercise faith and speak positivity into the universe. Don't waver from that, ever.

You are fearless! I admire that in you, and I want to keep that burning inside of you because that motivates me to be the best role model that I can be for you, every day. All that I do, say and show is for you and your brother. I want you two to support each other with love, support and stability.

You are now almost 14 years old and going to France. Seeing another part of the world has been a dream of yours since you were about nine years old, so, embrace, enjoy and have fun; that's what I want for you with this experience. I have dreamed this dream with you and for you.

Raising you is my pleasure and my honor. You are so unlike me in many ways, yet, so much like me in others. I just hope that my display of strength for you, guidance, and teaching make you as proud of me as I am of you.

Love,

Mom (Sandra)

Dear Daughters,

To my two beautiful daughters, my bonus (I hate the word "step") daughter and all the young women I've had the privilege to make an impact on. Being a mother and mentor can be the hardest of tasks, but also the most rewarding. I used to tell my girls, "You didn't come with a manual, so I'm doing the best I know how." I've made my fair share of mistakes but, all in all, I think I did ok. I've had the pleasure of sharing in your successes and hurts, the birth of my only grandchild (I got to cut the cord!) and just seeing you become the beautiful women that you are. I've shared my values, beliefs, opinions, successes and losses; and I know…I have a lot of opinions. I've always challenged you to be civic and community minded and to give back in the same way. You have been blessed, and there are so many others that have not had your blessings. Always vote; make your voice count!

I want you to never be afraid of being yourself; be real. Figure out your God-given gift, pursue it and then give it back to the world because God didn't give it to you solely for you. Always look to have multiple streams of income so if one dries up, you have others that will sustain you.

Don't ever define yourself by whether you have a man or not. It's worth waiting for that special one God has for you. When you do find him, I'll just give you some advice my mother gave me — start out the way you plan on ending up. This means that you should not try to be something you aren't just to get him, because if you change later, you will have a problem. If you want to make it to the end, faking it will be very hard. Lastly, always lead with love: love for God, yourself and others.

I'll always be your #1 fan,

Margo

In a mother's words…

"NEVER BE AFRAID TO BE YOURSELF."

Dear Zavi,

It's me, Tati! I was asked to write a letter to you and given no further instructions. You already know how "crazy" your Tat is, so I know you will understand every word I type.

As of right now, you are an amazing 6-year-old little girl. You are headstrong, confident, sassy, beautiful, talented and hardheaded. OMG, YOU ARE HARDHEADED! (LOL) These are just a few words to describe you; however, you are so much more than just these 6 "words."

I am aware that at 6, if you were to read this letter now, you wouldn't fully understand it. I do have confidence in knowing that when you are older and are thumbing through the pages of this book, you will understand each and every word (both written and unwritten).

Your Tati loves you and has loved you from the very beginning. I never thought I would love a kid as much as I love you. I also never thought that I would allow a child to touch my heart and soul in such a way that I would do anything within my power to keep her safe and happy.

Because of this, I know that you are spoiled and I acknowledge my contribution to that, at least to an extent. While my spoiling you won't change, I can't wait for you to learn and properly understand the difference between entitlement and necessity. The things I (we) do for you are not all things that have to be done in order for you to live. I know you think they are, and you are very adamant about it. (LOL) Again, you're only 6, but you will get there.

Please trust me, though, when I say that you will miss those naps that you fight so hard to not take. I live for the day that I call you to see how your day is and you tell me you're tired and just want a nap. I'm going to keep you on the phone for an entire hour! If you hang up on me, I'm going to keep calling you every 20 minutes about random stuff. Then, when you turn your phone off, I'm gonna show up at your house! I've got it all planned out honeychye…you just wait! *insert devilish laugh and the raised eyebrow you love so much*

I could write so much in this letter, but I feel as though I have gotten some of the important parts in. When I was about your age, my mommy said the following words to me and I have always remembered them and kept them in my heart. Even in her absence, I know that she still stands by her word and I want you to know that I feel the same exact way about you.

My sweet little Zav, "I want you to know that no matter where I am, I will always love you and be there for you. If you were to fall backwards, I would be behind you to catch you. If you were to fall forward, I would be right there in front of you. If you lean to the side, Tati will be right there to give you a shoulder to keep you balanced and off the ground."

In life, you will have some challenges, but things are only as hard as you make them. Always remember that you have me, you have us and before that, you have yourself. Love yourself and believe in yourself always, and you will conquer the world!

Forever yours,

Tati (Ronda)

P.S. GO TO SLEEP ZAVI!

To My Children:

Never make fun of having to help me with computer stuff. I had to teach you how to use a spoon.

Moms of the Universe.

My Dear Beverly,

You are 8 years old now and we're starting to venture into this new world of puberty. I haven't sat you down to start to fully describe it because, frankly, I'm still wrapping my mind around the fact that my 'baby' has a few hairs under her arms and her breasts are clearly starting to change. I asked your Grandma Joyce if she'd noticed these while you were staying at her house this summer and she said, "Yes, I did," which made me jokingly proclaim, "I'm not ready!"

That led to me and Grandma Joyce reminiscing about the times she sat me down and explained the way my body was changing. She gave me a book, which, while I don't remember the name, I do remember all the cartoonish pictures of boys' and girls' bodies going through the changes that come with puberty. I told her that I did buy a book, and gave her my rough outline of a plan on how I'm going to start talking with you about the more major changes you have yet to experience. We laughed about the ways I misunderstood some of what she told me and the mistakes I made stumbling through this period (and, ahem, MY period). She reassured me that while you'll probably misunderstand some of the things that I explain to you, just like I came through on the other side just fine, so will you.

When I was 8, my mom (your Grandma Beverly) was very ill and I was still fairly too young to have these talks, so they didn't happen. A year later, she would be dead, leaving your Pop-Pop trying to figure out how he would explain these things to me. Luckily, he had female friends to turn to (including your now Grandma Joyce), and they helped him out. Your Grandma Joyce told me what was going on and why. She helped me deal with this new stage of life. Your Aunt Sybil did the same, as did your Aunt Emmy. All of these women were ready to jump in to help your Pop-Pop as he dealt with the death of his wife and the reality of raising two girls. These women taught me a lot more than just how to cope with the physical and emotional changes of my body. They taught me how to be an independent, self-assured, caring and successful black woman.

I'm pretty sure I'll be around to have all the talks we need as you go through puberty. Yes, I'm a little freaked out. Yes, I may stumble through answering your questions. And yes, there may be questions that you wouldn't want to ask me. This is where I hope you look to all the black women you have in your life for assistance and answers. From your Aunty Amina and Aunty Jen to 'GG' Gloria and Grandma Joyce. These women love you and will support you, at all times, even if (or when) I am not up to the task or I am no longer physically around. I will be here anytime you need, for as long as I can, but also look to them for words of wisdom, and as role models, for what it is to be a strong black woman; loving fiercely, overcoming obstacles, achieving greatness in whatever they do. You have a circle of goddesses who will guide you along the way.

Jasmine

Dear Kayla,

As we quickly draw closer to your 23rd birthday, I thought there was no better time to convey both my love and adoration for you than now. As the woman who singlehandedly reared you (with the support of a great village), I have said throughout your life that I've been preparing you for these times where you could and would become a woman standing on her own, without me around very much, if at all.

I know that as a little girl, that was hard to hear. No child ever wants to think they wouldn't have their mom around, nurturing, spoiling and guiding them through life's obstacles. What I meant to convey and what you have come to fully embrace (in the last 60 plus days) is what it takes to be independent of me, so that you can live a good life on your terms.

This year, you've made me especially proud to be your mom. You graduated from college and you've managed to adapt and thrive since I departed the United States to live and work in China. All of this you've accomplished, without missing a beat or falling apart. If that does not speak volumes to the young woman you've become, then I don't know what else could. You've made my adaptation and adjustment to life without you here in Beijing just a little more bearable because you are doing so well. These are the days, the moments and times that all parents look forward to.

I miss you terribly but you now belong to the world; God first, the world second. I have done my job as a mom. I am proud of the results. You honor me every day by going to work, staying humble and continuously seeking to improve yourself. No greater joy will I ever know than my love for you. You are beautiful both inside and out. The blessings from God just radiate from you at all times and that's why everyone loves you. Keep doing great things!

The blessings are just beginning in this chapter of your life. Can't wait to see you at Christmas!

I love you forever!
Mom (Kaz)

To: The Replications of Every Good Thing That Is in Me,

You are so much more than this salutation, but that is the part of you that I am addressing. I am speaking to the parts of you that are me. The parts that were carved from God's spirit, poured from my soul and masterfully woven together into the complexity that is you. You were knitted together in my unconscious before you were ever a conscious thought; two sets of twenty-three chromosomes, a name on a birth certificate, safe in my arms. You were a level that my soul needed to reach, a height that my love needed to soar and a place that my dreams needed to live. I was your mother before I was ever a mother.

God purposed it so. You were my unfulfilled purpose before I knew what my purpose was. You are my destiny, my reason and my tomorrow. You are the gateway to a future that will exist long after my body has given up the ghost. I am the gateway to a past that ended before your life began. Together, we are a present force for love, peace, joy, kindness and good work. I write this letter to you three (Olayinka Indira, Imani Michelle, Isis Afia) as if I am writing to one, because for me, each of you is the most important piece of a whole that was incomplete before you were formed.

When I look in the mirror, I see you. When I look at you, I see me; I see my greatest accomplishments, my fullest joys and my biggest dreams. I smile when I see those parts of me. I also see the fear of rejection, abandonment, loneliness of my adolescence, foolish pride, stubbornness, isolation of my twenties and the parts of me that were afraid, sad, discouraged and broken in my thirties. I hurt when I see those parts of me, but I am quickly reminded that because I overcame all of those things, so shall you. I am confident that the same God that lives in me is ever present in you. The same God who loves me, loves you. The same God who saved me, will save you. The same God who healed me, will heal you. I am confident that you will see yourself the way that God sees you, you will be the women God purposed you to be and you will find that purpose for which you were created.

Despite that the world has problems, God makes no mistakes. As a matter of fact, He created you to solve it. The solution is inside of you. God knew exactly where to hide it in you and exactly what you needed from me to be inspired to find it. He knew what you needed to see in me in order to see Him in me so that you could see Him in you. You needed a mother who had survived rejection and learned that God's was the only acceptance that mattered; who had challenged her own pride and chosen humility; who had healed herself and refused to hide her scars. He also knew what I needed too; He knew that I needed you. The solution to a problem that the world has is hidden in me, too, and just like you needed to see me to find your purpose, I needed to see you to find mine. I needed you to see me overcome, to see me win, to see me change and to see me whole, so that I could walk in MY purpose.

So, Baby girls, please remember, there is nothing that you will encounter on this journey of life for which God has not already provided you with the strength to endure, the courage to face and the power to overcome in the pursuit of your life's purpose. He has implanted Himself inside your spirit and hidden the best parts of me inside your soul. So, when you look in the mirror, don't see the parts of me that were broken, but see the parts of me that were made whole for you. Smile when you see those parts of me.

I love you for always; in all ways,

Jacqueline B

In a mother's words…

"YOU WERE KNITTED TOGETHER IN MY UNCONSCIOUSNESS BEFORE YOU WERE EVER A CONSCIOUS THOUGHT…"

To My Daughters:

I may have only had you for a short while, but still, I feel blessed to have known you at all. I've always wanted a daughter. On November 18, 1986, I gave birth to my first child, a healthy little boy. At only 20 years old, I knew I wanted more than one child and that I'd try again for a little girl. It took a little longer than I expected but seven years later, I was finally pregnant again. My little girl was on her way. This I was assured of by every superstitious ritual and old wives' tale in the book of Black life. The shape of my belly, how I was carrying, how my chin creased when it was pinched, what foods I craved, and a 90-something-year-old woman's wrinkled hands all said, "Girl," with a capital G. Well, on September 8th, 1992, the time had finally come to meet her, my daughter…and to my surprise, I had another boy. A beautiful, plump little man child. I would turn 27 years old the week following my son's birth. What a wonderful gift!

As the years passed, I would never hold a daughter in my womb, but I would hold many in my heart. Believing as earnestly as I do in the African proverb, "It Takes a Village to Raise a Child," likewise, I believe that the little black girls who have lived in my home, heart and world are all my daughters. I've had daughters who have lived with me during the seven years that I was a foster parent; daughters who resided with me while grieving the loss of their own mothers, daughters that I mothered during times when I taught in middle and high schools, daughters who called me C.O. because they were incarcerated behind bars, daughters who I met as neighbors, and others that I met as a result of stepping onto a city bus or a crowded subway train…none of which called me mom, mommy or mother. They reserved those illustrious titles for the women whose wombs they had traveled through. However, many have confided in me, so much so that they secretly gave me maternal titles often, although most publicly referred to me as their foster parent, auntie, teacher, correction officer, the lady down the block, or simply, 'that woman on the train.'

In each and every relationship and encounter, I've tried to provide a safe space of comfort, guidance and sometimes, tough love; I've always wanted them to love themselves as much (if not more) than I have loved them.

As you might imagine, I've wished for them much of the love and life lessons my own biological mother has provided for me, and I've wished for them even more passionately, those things which my own mother could not provide. In doing so, I've learned so much.

I've learned that love and commitment extend far beyond biological connections, while learning how adhesive and potentially detrimental biologic bonds can often be. I've learned how important and expansive our reach is when we support each other, share knowledge and give each other permission to walk in our truths as Black women and Black female children. I've learned the importance of reminding you, my daughters, that your beauty is more than melanin deep, when that's all the rest of the world seems to notice — if they notice at all.

I've learned that life and growth is an ever-evolving process that's often painful, but never void of valuable lessons; that the journey to healing from some of the f*cked-up sh*t we go through in life is an ongoing and necessary excursion. More importantly, I've learned how much stronger we are together – whether I birthed you or not. So, thank you to all my daughters, for making me a better mother and a better me.

Sincerely,

Your Other Mother (L'Monique)

My #JoysOfJoule

I decided to name you Joule shortly after I found out that you were a girl. A joule is a unit of energy, and energy is something that cannot be created nor destroyed. That really summed up who I hoped you would be; full of life-giving energy, audacious, precocious, dynamic, free-spirited — a phenomenal Black girl-child.

So, from the very beginning, I have been purposeful in my parenting; always being honest with you, allowing you to ask questions about everything, and in turn, being open to explaining things to you as carefully as I could. I vowed to be dedicated to taking you everywhere and exposing you to diverse people and environments, while always attempting to use love, ancestral wisdom and reason to guide me along the way. And then, you turned three and a half.

You became increasingly opinionated and at times, down-right stubborn. A stubborn child is a force to be reckoned with; to be tamed by force — or by choice, many would say. But then again, I don't want to tame you. I don't want to extinguish that light inside of you that makes you unique. You are energy — beautifully alive, unpredictable and absolutely electrifying!

However, the reality is that there's a giant world out there; one beyond the safety of my arms, the calm of my voice, the watchful gaze of my eyes; a world that isn't always so kind to and accepting of little brown girls with eyes as bright as stars, and a spirit as wild and free as her tresses. Knowing that firsthand, I know that I also have to teach you to wrangle that energy at times.

You must be:

- self-aware so that you'll know when to code-switch and fit into a myriad of situations...
- mindful of rules to games that you can't choose to play but must...

- resilient in the face of hardships that will surely come your way…
- strong in ways that no one ever should be, but is expected of every Black woman and...

And there is the crux of it all. How do I help you stay electric without allowing you to fry everything in your wake? How do I guide you and also help you to remain free? How do I teach you to be obedient to both your mother and obedient to your intuition, both for your own good? Honestly, I'm not sure. I continue to parent in the ways I always have, but more than that, I question whether or not it's enough. So far, all I do know for sure is that you are Joule, so you can neither be created nor destroyed, and prayerfully, that will be foundation enough to make you phenomenal, as a woman.

Unique

Dear Ronda,

When you are reading this, I may not be around. Still know that you are (were) loved beyond my power (to the 100th power and more). Without you, I would not have had a life.

Forever Your Mom,

(La Vone - posthumous)

Dear Zavi,

I was there when you were born. I wasn't really there; I was in the lobby. I remember the first time I stayed with you by myself; that's when the guy was putting your bed together and you were watching every move he made. I remember the first time I held you, I almost dropped your head. Your head was rolling around. Frances had a good handle on you. I remember she used to make my daughter sing to you, and then you would try to sing too. You didn't make any sense, but you tried, and you could carry a tune, even though we couldn't understand what you were saying.

This is what I want you to remember:

- Zavi, you are a bright kid. You are smarter than you think you are.
- I was afraid of my mother for a long time. But eventually, I learned that she loved me.
- You'll always be special even if you don't think you are.
- Don't fight in school. Don't start the fight, but if someone is mean to you, defend yourself.
- Make sure you're doing the right thing.
- Don't lie. It's important to your relationship with your mother that you don't lie. She will believe everything you say if you don't lie.
- Watch out for the boys and the girls. Sometimes, they may make up stuff to win you over, and it isn't always true — check the source. Sometimes, they lie.
- Don't believe everything you hear. Check things out for yourself because everyone doesn't always mean well.
- Remember the tales you tell will catch up with you.

On Family:

- Remember your little cousin, Evangeline. Don't ever lie to her. Tell her the truth no matter how painful it is. Remember she relies on you for the truth.
- Don't be too hard on your father. Remember he was a kid once too.

On Spirituality:

Remember your connection to the Lord. Remember it solemnly. Ask your Mami and Tati how they pray. Ask your mother and Tati what they pray about, and what it means to them. Have faith in God and in God's presence. Never lose sight of that; never forget it. I've questioned His presence since childhood. I remember my mom spanked me one day because I didn't do something she told me to do. I remember praying that God would not let her whip me but God didn't intervene, and I had doubts about Him because of that. However, in the long run, I was able to understand what I was asking for.

It's been a great honor to be your Nana, and I dedicate this piece of work to you.

Bibi,

(Colesta; as dictated)

Dear LeAnna,

First, I give honor to God; thank You for Your mercy, love, and grace, because without you, where would l be? You, my child, know better than anyone where I've been and the journey it took to get here. I love you! You have grown up to be the best daughter a mother could have ever asked for. Your devotion to your family is undying.

Now, that being said, don't sweat the small stuff. Every battle isn't worth fighting. Enjoy life's treasures and all that it has for you. Believe in yourself; that oh-so-familiar voice you hear talking to you is God. Hold your tongue; that doesn't mean you should cower, but to think about what you say, in everything you do. As a parent, now, you're going to make mistakes. It's alright; she will live. There are things that as a single parent myself, I cannot teach you. Like relationships, you're on your own…maybe you can teach me something. LOL!!

Keep the lines of communication open with your village, and most of all, with your daughter, so that she will come to you first (even when she won't listen). You have a very diverse group of people around you. I'm proud of the selection of people that you have chosen to walk with you. I know we don't always agree on everything, but we are big enough to apologize and appreciate each other.

Hugs and kisses; you can't ever give enough. Say 'I love you' often, because I used to think I didn't say it enough. Protect her and do what is right for you both. Stop procrastinating. It doesn't look good on us. (SMILE) Now that you have a little one, it's important to teach her your values, not what's in those streets! I Love You, and you are doing a great job!

Love,

Your Mother (Shari)

In a mother's words...

"IT TAKES A VILLAGE TO RAISE A CHILD."

Hey baby girl,

I'm writing because I just want to open up and tell you the sentiments of my heart. It is so painful for me to witness the struggle you are going through right now. But no matter how dark and bleak it seems, just hold on because your change is coming and eventually, it will come. If it's alright with you, I'd like to share some of the intimate details of my journey with depression and mental illness.

When I was your age, I was attending the University of Washington. My new found freedom and the vast size of campus got the better of me. Prioritizing everything except for my class work caught up with me. I had no idea of the help and resources that could have assisted in getting me out of the rut and the hole that I had dug for myself. So, to save face, I quit school and found myself a full-time job before anyone figured out that I wasn't going back to school the next fall. That was when depression first reared its ugly head. I had no idea what it was and just figured I was a moody, opinionated, vocal, didn't-give-a-damn young woman. My depression was cyclical. There were times when I was extremely productive, but then I would eventually wind down and feel sick. My coping mechanism was being home on the couch, ordering pizza and drinking orange Fanta until I would feel better.

In February 1996, I found out that I was pregnant with you, and in March, my daddy passed away. You kept me balanced and sane during an extremely difficult time in my life. But, I put off mourning your grandfather's death until after you were born, and I was certain that you were alright.

The day before you turned a year old, I wanted to do my 'pizza and orange Fanta' ritual and cry myself to sleep, but I looked at your beautiful smiling face and realized that there was no way I could give in to a shutdown. In front of me was a little being that was dependent on me. I had to do something different.

After 15 years of trial and error, I got on Prozac and finally gained some stability. Through therapy, I learned how to battle the voices in my head that kept telling me that I wasn't smart enough, pretty enough, good enough, etc. Finally, I was able to have some clarity of thought and moved forward. Unfortunately, once I felt fine, I quit my meds.

You would see the times I had energy and felt like I could rule the world, but unfortunately, you saw more of the shut-in recluse. For this, I am so sorry that I wasn't as present in your life as I should have been. It breaks my heart, and I feel awful that I couldn't be as engaged as you deserved me to be. Please forgive me, Nia.

Now, I know that I will probably take these meds for the rest of my life, but I'm okay with that. If I was a diabetic, no one would dare tell me to come off my insulin without doctor's guidance, and suggest that I could be healthy otherwise. This chemical imbalance isn't any different than the imbalance of serotonin, norepinephrine, or any of the other neurotransmitters in my brain. A good therapist and learning new coping mechanisms have given me life.

So, baby girl, I want you to be encouraged. I would go through all of this again just to know that I would be able to reach out and help my beloved child make her way through her journey. I love you, Nia. You will conquer this. You will make it to the other side of healthy.

Love you much, much more than mostest,

Mommy (Myrna)

To my only, miracle child,

First off, I'll start by saying THANK YOU for loving me unconditionally. Wow, where do I begin? Being your mother has been an unbelievable experience. When I was 16, I was told that I couldn't have children; the doctor told me I had Dysplasia (determined from a pap smear). I had never heard of it or knew what it was. It's a precancerous condition in which an abnormal cell growth occurs on the surface lining of the cervix or endocervical canal. I had no symptoms and, to this day, I have no idea how I obtained it.

I had a LEEP which stands for Loop Electrosurgical Excision Procedure. It's a treatment that prevents cervical cancer. In this procedure, a small electrical wire loop is used to remove abnormal cells from your cervix. So, when I say that you're a "Miracle Baby," you live up to that. Each day, I thank God for placing you in my life. I had been so lonely until I became your mother.

The love you have shown me over these past 11 years has been the greatest love I've felt in all my 25 years of living (inside joke). LOL! It's one thing to be told you're loved, but actually feeling it is a different story. I've been through so much heartache in my life that it almost ruined me, but God blessed me with you, and that is what keeps me going. You're such an inspiration and I am pretty sure you know it. I try not to only tell you, but show you how much you mean to me. I'm so elated to have the relationship that I couldn't have with my parents with you. I constantly tell you that I don't always do things right, or know everything, but regardless, you don't even abuse or mistreat me when I don't. You have helped me in so many ways that you may not have imagined. I am a better woman, mother, friend and much more because of you.

I will ALWAYS promise to put you first after God, of course, because I am so grateful for the gift that He has blessed me with. I vow to protect you, even if it takes my own life. We've been through a lot together and it's a miracle we're both here. I am glad you know that you can always count on me and come to me for just about anything. That's so important to me because I didn't have that. Everything I didn't have, I'm making sure that you do, so that you won't ever have the feelings and/or experiences that I've had. Communication and relationships are so important to me. I pray that I continue to be the best mother/role model for you. I love you with EVERYTHING in me! Keep believing and trusting in me…it has a supernatural effect on me.

Signing off as:

Your Mother/Best Friend/ Ride or Die! (Rita)

To my dearest Laila,

I want you to realize that there will be times when you fail. You can't be afraid of failure because it happens to anyone who tries at some point. Success can only happen when you try.

I have always been a bit of a perfectionist, and so, school came easy. I made the decision to be a doctor at the age of 5, when someone suggested that "girls aren't doctors, they're nurses." I told that person that I WOULD be a doctor. That desire was solidified in the eighth grade with the death of a classmate from bone cancer. After that, I took efforts to position myself towards that goal. I took advanced classes, went to science and pre-medical camps, left home 2 years early to go to a special boarding school for math/science and selected what I thought to be the best college to get me into medical school. I thoroughly enjoyed my undergraduate years, but that's a story for another letter. My grades were average in college. I worked and had multiple extracurricular activities. I likely over-extended myself. My standardized test scores were above average for the nation, but average for my college. My premed counselor tried to steer me towards social work or a PhD in science, saying that I might not be suited for medicine.

In spite of all the odds stacked against me, I applied to medical school. I was destined to be a doctor, despite signs that things were not lining up perfectly. At graduation, when everyone else knew where they were going, my future was uncertain. I went back home to my parents' house, got a temporary job at the bank, and waited to get off of the waitlist for the one school that did not say no. I did not get off the waitlist. To say I was devastated would be an understatement. My mother, meaning well, told me it was ok, and that we were just a family of failures. I now know that she was expressing her own feelings of failure in an effort to make me feel better, but I never knew she felt that way, and I refused to accept failure. We were NOT a family of failures. I moved back to my college town, got a job doing medical research and applied the next year and, again, was put on the waitlist. One school suggested I apply for their post-baccalaureate program because, it would help to strengthen my application. They sounded confident that I would get in after that. I applied to the post-bacc program, and they rejected me. They said my application was 'too strong' for their post-bacc program and that I should apply directly to the medical school, which I did the following year; well, they rejected me again. People I knew from out of state were getting into MY instate schools before me. People with worse grades who had the advantage of the booster programs got in before me. Frustrated and broken-hearted, I decided to move on with my life. I got married to your father and moved to a new city to start our lives together. I continued doing medical research. We bought a house on a cul-de-sac and got a puppy. I settled into life in research and as a wife, but my dream was still there.

Then something happened — an awakening. I was not challenged by my job; it bored me. I realized I was only happy when I was talking to patients as a part of my job. Your dad got a raise that was more than my salary. I decided to try one more time, and this time, I extended my net to schools farther from home. One of the schools I applied to was Indiana University School of Medicine. I had never been to Indiana, but one of my sorority sisters had gone there, and our grades were similar. I didn't want to go, neither did I want to spend the money. Your father insisted and bought the ticket. During my interview, the interviewer's radio played Mariah Carey's song, "Hero," which was a song I would sing to myself all of the time. I took it as a sign; it was. I got in, we moved to Indiana, and the rest is history.

Now, I am a respected and well-known physician in the community. I have won an award as a top doctor in the city, voted by my peers. I'm currently the medical director at my clinic. I don't say these things to brag, but to revel in how far I have come from those dark days when I was struggling to get into medical school; when it looked like my dream would be deferred. I say this to you, my beautiful, driven, ambitious daughter, because you are more like me than you know. You will be successful, but you will also fail. Your failures do not have to define you. Use them as lessons because there is ALWAYS a lesson. Take the lesson and keep moving forward. It is also ok to change your mind. Go with your gut and what feels right. If your original goal no longer feels right, change it. Sometimes, that is the lesson. My gut told me that I was put here to help people as a doctor, and my gut was not wrong.

Love,

Mom (Ajiri)

In a mother's words...

"YOUR FAILURES DO NOT HAVE TO DEFINE YOU. USE THEM AS LESSONS; BECAUSE THERE IS ALWAYS A LESSON."

My Dearest Zoe,

I don't find it surprising that today is October 4th; you've turned four years old and I'm sitting here, typing up a letter, sharing just how much you mean the world to me. My Daughter, my baby girl, Zoe Doll Harrison, the apple of my eye. Zoe means 'life,' and that's exactly what you have given us; your Mommy and I. You never cease to amaze us. It was four years ago today, in the evening, I sat there, waiting on the edge of my seat for you to make your entrance while comforting your other Mommy as she laid there in pain.

Giving birth to you will always be the greatest gift she could ever give us. Having a miscarriage from the previous pregnancy devastated us. Your brother would have been 6 years old this year. The pain was unimaginable; some days, I would lay in bed, wondering how I would get out of there.

This experience not only drew Mommies closer to each other, but also, to God. It was an experience that taught us to cast all of our cares on God. He was a present help in the time of a great need; a need to regain my thinking, because there were times that I felt like I couldn't.

You turned 4 and I turned 44 this year. You have truly been my dream come true. You have completed me as a mother. You have fulfilled my number one purpose in life. Thank you for being more than I could have ever expected.

Mommy and I have dedicated you back to God, and we promise to teach you and expose you to everything we can think of to enhance your life. We travel the world not just to take a vacation, but also, to expose you to different walks of life and different cultures of people.

We are instilling in you the value of love and respect to everyone, no matter where they come from, no matter their outer appearance. Personally, I will teach you not to be gullible or naïve. People will try to take advantage of people with a heart like yours. I will protect you when I can, but more importantly, I will always cover you in prayer.

God is your ultimate protector. Your mind is already beyond your little four years. There isn't anything you cannot achieve. Your natural competitive nature will get you far in life. You will be amazed when you get older how much of your life we have captured, and all of the memories we have made. You will always know and feel how much we love you. No matter my experiences, lessons, trials or tests, life is great, just because you're a part of it.

I love you, Zoe,

Mommy (Tiffany)

Camille & Cydney,

My Loves, words cannot express how much it excites me every day to know that I am your mother. When I think about having the opportunity to be able to teach, show and provide you with experiences that shape you as women, I am humbled.

I can remember watching you both while you slept when you were infants, and believe it or not, I still watch you even though you are 12 and 8 years old. The two of you have brought so much joy into my life. It's hard for me to watch you grow up so fast. I want to enjoy every minute that we have together.

You mean so, so much to me. As you continue to grow, there will be situations that may arise where I may become angry or upset with you. This is only because I want the best for you. I want you to be able to learn from your mistakes and learn to question how to improve on the things that matter to you most. I don't want you to experience some of the things that I have or make some of the same mistakes I made.

I will have to ask for a little patience from you because as you grow and gain more of your independence, I will have to learn to let you explore a little more without me. It is hard for me now, and I can't imagine that it will get any easier. I know that I cannot shield you from all of the bumps and bruises of life. Believe it or not, those experiences can strengthen you and push you to be an even better person.

I really want the two of you to live your lives. See and experience all that you can. There are so many cities and countries to visit. Please don't allow anyone to convince you that time is on your side and you can do it later. Go as often as you are able to. Pace yourself in a manner that will allow you to set a strong foundation and to ensure that you can enjoy your adventures without having concerns when you return.

There will be people that may come into your lives and try to distract you from loving who you are. You are beautiful young ladies, and you are to be respected. Know this, and know that you are enough! I hope that you learn from me that your family is very important, and as sisters, your bond should be cherished. I know that you may not feel that way right now, but one day, you will become best friends.

Last but not least, know that I will ALWAYS have your back.

I Love You,

Mom (Charlenea)

Dearest Daughters:

I could not have imagined that God would have blessed me with my dream and wish of having twins! I remember as a teen, wanting twins when I became a mother. Through the years, I've heard more times than not that I "must be crazy" to want, not one, but two children at the same time. If only they knew and could understand the joy of having two beautiful little ones to love, nurture and watch grow into the lovely women that you are today. I had no idea what joy I would have every day of my life, starting at birth, then, when you were infants, toddlers, school age, etc. I would not change a single thing!

In accepting this gift from God, I promised that you'd always be close to one another, be each other's protector (when Daddy and I are not there) and love one another as we loved you. But I NEVER imagined how close you two would be, until the time(s) came that where I would talk to one, and the other one would speak. Well, my conversation would instantly be put on 'hold.' I would feel some kind of way, but marveled at the good job I was doing in guiding you to keep each other first. I enjoyed watching you two be your own playmates (never had to worry about someone being your friend!). I've never been one for attention, but boy, did that change! We couldn't go anywhere without you two being the center of attention from family or strangers, in passing.

After you grew older and shared the stories of how you would 'trick' your teachers, all I could do was laugh and say, "Good job," because that's what identical twins are supposed to do (or at least try it).

As women with families of your own, I admire your dedication and convictions to your family's wellbeing. I admire your maturity in all that you set out to accomplish, and your honesty, no matter what the situation.

It warms me to see you following the major things that I've instilled in you from youth; planting your feet firmly on the ground when you stand because you belong here, and ALWAYS walking with your head up!

If I was called home to glory today, I would have a smile on my face because of you, my first loves. You have made me the woman that I am, and have given me so MUCH joy. Happiness is easy, but having joy is a reward with no end.

My love and adoration are infinite,

Mommy (Mary)

In a mother's words…

"I THOUGHT I WAS HERE TO RAISE YOU, BUT YOU RAISED ME."

Dear Shari,

To be asked to write a letter to my daughter at this time in my life, the most I can say is, "Thank you, God, for Shari!" The things that I wanted for her as a young mother can't compare to the joy that she has given me in my seasoned years.

I wanted her to find a godly man that loved her, have a few children and live life according to God's word. Things didn't go that way…but God took my mistakes and turned them into a daughter that is beautiful, strong, loving, giving, humble and wise. God turned her into a daughter that a lot of people wished they had.

What do I wish for my daughter? As it turns out, she has given me more than I have ever given her. Yes, I birthed her but there is no way I could have put all that she is into her unless God hadn't.

As a young woman, I didn't know what I was doing but I knew that I loved children and wanted to raise them to be whole adults, able to stand on their own two feet and help others stand, if needed. I saw my parents devote their lives to family, even above their own happiness. I didn't want to give up my life to raise children and have no fun.

I started getting rewards and payback sooner than I thought. That is why I say, "Why ask me, now?" My daughter has given me love that many can't buy. Shari has supported, helped me to be a mature woman and helped me grow into a person that others love.

I still want her to find a godly man that loves God, her and her family. I want them to travel and have fun together for the rest of her life. After the children go to bed, I want her to have someone to talk to, hold hands with, go places with, smile at in love, laugh about the day's journey and share paying the bills (smile).

I want God to forgive my sins and for me to forgive those that have hurt me, for they didn't know what they had done. We are going to make mistakes, but don't be too proud to ask for forgiveness. Work on good relationships; some people have gone through a lot in their lives. Trust that God's will is best for your life.

Shari, out of all the daughters, God gave me the very, very best! Happiness is peace of mind! I love how she redirected her life after the illness which caused her to stop working. She had a hard time, but she didn't give up, and she let God work it out. You must go to the Lord in prayer for your needs! God will never leave or forsake you! It takes a village!

I love you,

Mama (Georgia Ann)

Dear Rachel,

When I think about what I have to be grateful for, it is you and Matt. I have been fortunate, in that, I have been a part of the most part of your life. You have had many challenges, even more successes, and you know that I am proud of you.

My wishes for you this year are that you: (I know you may be doing some/all of this)

- Stay true to yourself - Remember that others may or may not agree with your path, but you are the one that has to live it.
- Live an honorable life – It does matter what you do when no one is looking.
- Reach out and connect with others in your life. I know that this seems to be a challenge for you, but there are others that want and need to hear from you.
    - Your brother has had some life-changing events and has taken some positive steps to address his future. Check on him periodically, Rachel.
    - Reach out to your grandmother – She is 92 years old and is struggling with several things (age, arthritis, etc.). She would love to hear from you.
- Take good care of your body. You only have one, and many things as you know, cannot be replaced. You can eat and live well without spending a fortune.
- Be optimistic – Believe it until it happens.

Some time ago, I read this note and thought of you. I thought I would share it with you, along with my comments about each statement:

- Don't hold onto hurt, anger, people you don't love and those who don't love you back. Worry will kill you, so will hurt and anger. Nothing grows more malignant with time than bad feelings. Let go of people and experiences that have caused you pain. Move on and live in peace.

- Take chances. As parents, we spend so much time and effort trying to protect our kids. It is important to learn from mistakes, grow from failure and build confidence through success.
- Same-sex marriage, abortion, health care and religion. Don't vote into law or argue with others about choices that are not yours to make. On the other hand, help pass laws that promote fairness.
- You are in no way obligated to follow in the footsteps of either parent. Although I've brought you up free of religion, you may find that life with God is better than life without. The choice will be yours. I will be proud of you no matter where you land on the spectrum of belief.
- Whatever you do, please remember that every text you send, every email you write, every picture you post, can surface later, at any time. Don't let yourself down, neither should you let others you know and love down.
- Stay in touch!
- If you use a credit card, pay it off every month without fail. Wait 3 days to make a purchase, which will help you avoid emotional or impulse purchases.
- Don't expect life to be fair, for things to even out in the end or to get your just desserts. Life is far less fair than what you have experienced. Things don't really even out, and you don't get what you deserve. Sometimes, you get more. Sometimes, you get less. You're not entitled to anything except respect from others. You will have both home runs and strikes, but don't quit. Life does not reward natural talent or intelligence or beauty. You will be rewarded for a positive attitude, for your competence, but most of all, for your grit.
- I see a lot of academic dishonesty, and I know you saw it as a student. If you take words, answers or even values from

others, then you are nothing more than a receptacle. Don't be a container for everyone else's junk. Be your own work of art.

- The underpinning of treating others well is treating ourselves well, too; we cannot give love and respect that we do not have. Don't hurt yourself with too much food or drink. Be the woman who does the right thing and who is fair; but also, be sure that you are fair to yourself.
- These things you already know, but it doesn't hurt to repeat: Always look people in the eye, offer a firm handshake, show up on time, help out, be present. Your phone is not a person – pay attention to those around you. Don't text and drive – keep others safe too. It's OK to discriminate, as long as it is based on behavior. Don't be tolerant of disrespect.

Rachel, I know you are searching for your own answers, but if you ever need an ear or a shoulder, have a question or a problem, I'm here; always, no matter how far you go in distance or time. Even adults reach out. It's not a sign of weakness but of strength. Enjoy every moment.

There is no grand prize at the end of your life, no all-expense paid trip to Utopia. This is your final destination. The prize is here, now, in every breath you take, every new friend, every kiss, every challenge, every exciting piece of information you discover.

Merry Christmas Rachel.

Love,

Mom (Susan)

To: Seairra, Shakeya, Courtney (My 3 Beautiful Daughters)

As I write this letter, I'm reminded of just how special each one of you are in your own unique way. I've watched you all grow into Beautiful Young Ladies, and I'm so proud of you all.

SEAIRRA: My first baby girl. When you told me your dreams of being in the fashion industry as a stylist, I was so excited. Yes, fashion, that is you; everything about you says so. What does your heart say? My gem for you is: Going forward, don't let anything or anyone stop you from getting your heart's desires. Keep your mind and your heart on your dreams. To thine own self be true!

SHAKEYA: My middle baby girl, bold and outspoken, hard, and doesn't take any mess from anyone; because of this, I didn't worry about you as much. You mirror me more than any of my other children. Now that you are a mother, I see a softer side of you; your strength and courage amaze me. My gem to you is: With the heart of a mother, see the world. Your beautiful smile will open doors for you; however, a soft heart will keep it open to you. To thine own self be true!

COURTNEY: My baby girl, my 7th child. Wow, we are so close, and I guess this is because the 3 oldest had each other, the 3 boys had each other and all you were left with was me. I clung to you because I didn't want you to grow up lonely. Now, look at you living the college life; "you go girl!" I'm so proud of you. My gem to you is: Don't stop, keep pushing, keep pursuing and keep believing in yourself. To thine own self be true!

I have had some hard times in my life. There was a time when I didn't even want to live; there have also been times when I didn't know how I could even go on living. There were many nights I stayed up crying, not knowing how I was going to make it through another day but I never gave up. How could I, when I had children, especially my girls? I remember praying and asking God to not let my daughters go through the pain and hurt that I went through.

I've always wanted only the best for you. I wish I could protect you from all of life's ills, but I can't.

However, what I can do is be a living example for you; of a woman of strength, in that, in spite of all I've been through, I never gave up. I kept praying, crying and holding on working to better myself, always believing that one day, I would be better. So, even now, at the age of fifty-one, I will keep moving forward and pursuing my dreams, while always looking at the world with the heart of a mother and believing in myself.

My Gem: All things are possible through Jesus Christ who strengthens. To thine own self be true!

Tawanna

To: My Daughter

If you only knew how much I love you.

If you only knew the sadness I felt when your dad didn't honor the little girl that I was raising you to be. Although you were always stubborn, I looked at it as a strength. I figured that one way or another, you will get a lesson from it; it's either it will push you to be your best, or show you how strong you really are.

If only you knew how proud of you I am. Your first name before your given name was DAUGHTER. The Pride I hold in that is beyond words. I would be the first person you would see as a role model, provider and leader. You changed my life because I only wanted to show you greatness, with flaws, of course. I wanted you to see me fall, but get back up.

Your strength, grace and ability to find the good in people is a gift; and you get it, honestly. The curse in that is the way you take ownership of the load. Remember, your gift misused (or abused) will rob you of the experience you earlier envisaged. I wish I could save the innocence that you carried and give it out in small doses, but I can't.

Instead, I pray your strength gets you through hard times. When the unspoken shame steps in, I pray that you see the growth and not the shame. I pray the same small glimmer of hope that you see in every other individual, you see in yourself as well. Don't be so hard on yourself when looking back; it will then seem small. I hope your determination to prove someone wrong helps you and does not harm you.

You are a smorgasbord of talent. You are great at many things, and I hope you continue to create. Love is your downfall because it consumes you. You take time to learn them; but you forget about yourself. Remember what you bring to the table. Remember, you are queen in your house. Don't forget that you are the definition of balance. You've had to be that all of your life for your brothers… and in appreciation, they show you that you are royalty. They've opened doors for you, brought you flowers and always protected you, even when you didn't want it. I pray that you remember that in your relationships with men. Remember the men who honor you. Examples were put in place for you as a guide map. The map goes where you go.

I wish that you could feel my heartbeat in every adventure you take on. Stay as brave as I am in all you do. Most of all love, I hope you feel love because you are loved. There will be times when you will experience loneliness, just know that you are not alone and that God is there; you will miss the blessing if you focus on the loneliness. Let God use you. I only know that from my own experiences. You learn more about yourself when it's just you. It can feel scary, but know that God has you covered.

Loosen up! You can only see one day at a time. You will only stress yourself out trying to do God's work. Leave that up to him/her; the biggest thing is to grow. Listen to your inner 'Nos' and don't ignore them. You can always change your mind if it doesn't feel right. Second-guessing yourself is really just you being ok with the wrong choice; your first choice is right. Your first choice simply wasn't justified one million times. It was a feeling that came naturally. That gut is God. Be the woman that you want your child to emulate. Don't be scared of life, LIVE IT! Be bold. You don't always have to play it safe... give room to dream big. Do what you fear. Give it a shot, so you won't be left to wonder what could have been. I hope you feel the love in this letter because I prayed over every sentence.

With all that I am, I LOVE YOU!

Love,
Mommy (Iesha)

In a mother's words…

"DON'T BE SCARED OF LIFE…LIVE IT!"

The contents of this letter were dictated to me by my mom who is in the late stages of Alzheimer's. As she had lucid moments, I was able to get the following from her. While her delivery may have been skewed, her message is clear:

To my Dearest Daughters and Granddaughter,

I look at your pictures often and selfishly wish I were with you. I want you to know how often you are in my thoughts and prayers. I've been thinking about the various changes that need to happen around here, and I know things are in the works, all in God's timing. One thing I know for sure is, if you and your sister were here, you would get the job done.

I am so blessed to have a granddaughter. She brightened my life and, Lord knows, I've always wanted a grandchild. Zavi is so smart, funny, independent, caring, thoughtful, helpful and she loves God. Cayme, thank you for her.

A few things for each of you to remember in life...

- God will always provide you with many blessings and unmatched favor.
- Have fun in life.
- Don't be afraid to be silly.
- Don't have children unless you're willing to put in the work.
- Get a Job. Find something that you like doing and make money doing it; don't settle for just anything. Make sure you are being paid what you're worth.
- You have the power to change your situation.
- Have a firm spiritual foundation.
- Let God guide you in your relationships; platonic and romantic ones.

- Follow God's Divine purpose for your life. You also have to make sure you are listening and paying attention to the messages.
- Don't allow people to walk all over you.

Love,

Mommy/Grammy (Audrey)

Dear Zavi,

It is so important to me that you know you came from love. Oftentimes, I tell you how much I prayed for you and manifested your very existence because I wanted a little girl — because I wanted you. You are not on this earth by accident. There is a very special light inside of you - we all have it - and I get excited every time you allow that light to shine bright. Please don't ever dim your light for any reason. Your world is full of light and love. You have intentionally been surrounded with people who love you unconditionally. When you are old enough to choose your circle, be wise with who you let in. It's ok to set boundaries that protect you, your light, your peace, and your energy.

Please don't ever forget this: you are enough exactly how you are, being authentically who you are. There is nothing that is flawed about you. The way you are is enough to do what you were put on this earth to do. The sooner you can understand that you are enough, and at the same time, allow yourself room to evolve into better versions of yourself, the happier and more content you will be in life. You are one of my greatest blessings.

BIG Love,

Mami (Cayme Andrea)

P.S. Remember what you wrote on the board in my office: "Walk in your own path, NOT someone else's, just so that what happens to them won't happen to you." You were only nine, but these are words to live by.

To You, Reader:

You made it to the last letter, written just for you!

Listen, no matter where you are in your life, one thing that I know for sure is that you can be stifled by what I like to call 'headtrash.' This is when you let thoughts that don't serve you take up precious real estate in your mind. Understand this, anonymous daughter of the Universe, your thoughts aren't true. Much of what you think about yourself, your life and other people is a result of your life experiences and assumptions you've never chosen to question. Without getting too deep, just know that simply because you think a thing, doesn't mean it's the truth. If you don't believe me, try this with the next thought you have that doesn't serve you: Ask yourself, "how do I know that to be true?" and keep asking until you realize that somewhere along the way, you made an assumption of what you thought to be true.

You have the power to choose a different thought. You can choose the thought that serves you and act on that. Your headtrash is keeping you from living the life that you were designed to live. Even if you've done well for yourself, there is still an opportunity for you to evolve into a better version of you; there is still room for you to impact more people, and impact them on a deeper level.

The word "love" was mentioned 200 times in this book. I believe that's because the biggest life lesson for you to learn is to love yourself; then, you can love others in a healthy way. Your headtrash prevents you from loving yourself in a deep, unapologetic way. This translates to you allowing people, places and situations that don't serve your highest good to exist in your space. You teach people how to treat you by how you treat yourself. So, it's imperative that you learn this. It took me being verbally and emotionally abused and then physically assaulted by someone who claimed to love me for me to get it. Daughter, please don't learn this lesson the hard way. That experience birthed and solidified the 4 Rules of Engagement® that I live by:

- Love Fiercely.
- Forgive Quickly.
- Do No Harm.
- Take No Shit.

But understand, it starts with you! Master the 4 Rules with yourself first. It will help clear the headtrash and make it easier to set healthy boundaries with others. I may never have met you, but we come from the same Source, and that Source is Love. It is your right, it is your privilege, and it is your responsibility to be the best, brightest and boldest extension of that Love as much as possible!

In love,

Coach Cayme Andrea

AFTERWORD

We want to hear from you. We encourage you to respond with your impressions, observations, thoughts, and ideas about your journey through this book. If there is a submission that particularly struck you, we'd love to hear that too!

If you, or anyone you know, would like to participate in the next compilation, get in touch with us using the information below.

Contact information:
hello@caymeandrea.com
www.caymeandrea.com

Made in the USA
Coppell, TX
05 May 2022